W9-AJU-207

Thomas Kinsella

LITTLEBODY

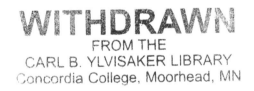
Peppercanister 23

Peppercanister

Distributed in Ireland by
The Dedalus Press,
24 The Heath, Cypress Downs, Dublin 6W

in the United Kingdom by
Carcanet Press Limited,
4th Floor, Conavon Court,
12-16 Blackfriars St., Manchester M3 5BQ

in the United States & Canada by
Dufour Editions Inc.,
P.O.Box 7, Chester Springs, Pennsylvania 19425

First published December 2000

The Dedalus Press
ISBN 1 901233 70 7 (paper)
ISBN 1 901233 71 5 (bound)

Carcanet Press Ltd
ISBN 1 85754 532 X (paper)
ISBN 1 85754 533 8 (bound)

Printed in Ireland by Colour Books Ltd.

The Dedalus Press receives financial support from
The Arts Council, An Chomhairle Ealaíon, Dublin.

Littlebody

Down Survey (1655-1657)

The young men chanted beside the public way :

Is there any sorrow like ours
who have forfeited our possessions
and all respect?

And the virgins of the Parrish of Killmainham

hung down their heads.

CONTENTS

Breakdown

Onset of restlessness and confusion,
and mental absences settling in disorder.

With a coarsening of the personality
— the exaggeration of established traits —

and an infantile stubbornness :
interests narrowed to the self,
irritation the dominant mood,
and ceaseless indiscriminate demands on others.

Shop Shut

I pulled the heavy door over
and leaned my head against it,
    the long key coarse in my face.

Inserted the iron teeth in the box lock
and turned the heart of the handle
    on my den of images. Shop shut.

Summer night, Percy Lane.
The last light full of midges.
    Gnats out of nothing.

Glenmacnass

I

I have known the hissing assemblies.
The preference for the ease of the spurious
— the measured poses and stupidities.

On a fragrant slope descending into the smoke
over our foul ascending city
I turned away in refusal,
holding a handful of high grass
sweet and grey to my face.

II

A light deer sailing back and forth
up the hill through the long grass
on his accurate feet

stopped to look back at the mess
scattered at our back door,
and disappeared in among the trees.

III

Pet before breakfast :
on her back,
in her morning affair with my bare foot

ribs frail
silk paw
pearl fang.

IV

We sat face to face at the kitchen table
our cups empty.

Outside, a voice from a black throat
passing high overhead in the light,
and a coarse, quiet throat-answer.

Two crows flying over to their place
on the far side of the valley.

V

I left the road where a stile entered the quiet wood.
Dry trees standing in order in their own grain.

Close up, on a patch of bark, a mouse body.
Upside down. Wings flat.

Meant only to be half seen
quick in the half light : little leather angel
falling everywhere, snapping at the invisible.

VI   *Littlebody*

Up on the high road, as far as the sheepfold
into the wind, and back. The sides of the black bog channels
dug down in the water. The white cottonheads
on the old cuttings nodding everywhere.
Around one more bend, toward the car shining in the distance.

From a stony slope half way, behind a rock prow
with the stones on top for an old mark,
the music of pipes, distant and clear.

*

I was climbing up, making no noise
and getting close, when the music stopped,
leaving a pagan shape in the air.

There was a hard inhale,
a base growl,
and it started again, in a guttural dance.

I looked around the edge
— and it was Littlebody. Hugging his bag
under his left arm, with his eyes closed.

I slipped. Our eyes met.
He started scuttling up the slope with his gear
and his hump, elbows out and neck back.

But I shouted :
                    "Stop, Littlebody!
I found you fair and I want my due."

He stopped and dropped his pipes,
and spread his arms out, waiting for the next move.
I heard myself reciting :

"Demon dwarf
with the German jaw,
surrender your purse
with the ghostly gold."

He took out a fat purse,
put it down on a stone
and recited in reply, in a voice too big for his body :

"You found me fair,
and I grant your wishes.
But we'll meet again,
when I dance in your ashes."

He settled himself down once more
and bent over the bag,
                    looking off to one side.

"I thought I was safe up here.
You have to give the music a while to itself sometimes,
up out of the huckstering

— jumping around in your green top hat
and showing your skills
with your eye on your income."

He ran his fingers up and down the stops,
then gave the bag a last squeeze.
His face went solemn,

his fingertips fondled all the right places,
and he started a slow air

               out across the valley.

*

I left him to himself.
And left the purse where it was.
I have all I need for the while I have left

without taking unnecessary risks.
And made my way down to the main road
with my mind on our next meeting.

Cul de Sac

Going Home

It was getting late.
The cousins were pulling at everything
and only playing with each other.

It was a long walk home
beside the baby's pram
with the two of them arguing all the way.

Under the high railway arch.
Into our own street in the dark.
And getting the pram up the front step.

She lit the lamp inside without a word
and I knew it was the start
of another long hate.

Holy Well

Our hands over our faces,
     making our promises.
A bench of senior boys out of St. Canice's.

          *

We leaned our bicycles against a farm wall
     and I took my turn, kneeling in the stone dark
to drink the holy water.

We stood there and wiped our mouths afterwards,
     talking for a while
after the cold kiss.

Cul de Sac

It was late at night,
and the neighbourhood unfamiliar after so long.
I took a turn too soon

and pulled in beside a terrace of grey houses
across from the windows of my old school,
with the double-fronted disused house closing the street.

A man lying in the headlights
in a black soutane at the foot of the steps,
with his arm across his face.

The Body Brought to the Church

Her voice on the phone was remote,
but familiar from long ago.

*

Round one more corner, by old habit,
I found St. Agnes's.
                    The entrance full of relatives :
cousins, in elderly excitement,
introducing wives and husbands.

I looked around for the older sister.
But no one had called about her. It was always
himself and myself, born the same time.

We took our places inside, around the church,
kneeling and sitting back
and noticing each other here and there.

A bell rang, and a young priest appeared
from around the side of the altar. He began
by praising the deceased as a good husband
and good father and friend in the neighbourhood.
Then consoled the bereaved,
ending the pious phrases with a modest flourish.

He stepped to one side, and his place was taken
by a young parishioner, moustached and heavy,
who spoke with directness and love.
A son and friend of the dead.

Others followed, daughters and another son,
remembering him and assembling around the coffin.

Lines of mourners formed in the side aisles,
approached the priest, accepted the Host in turn,
and turned away, back toward their places.

The service ended with the gesture of peace
around the congregation. The girl beside me
took my hand in both of hers with a smile.

The sons and daughters led the congregation
down the centre aisle toward the front door,
and we joined the end of the procession as it passed.

Outside, when the family were driven away,
we mixed again in the same friendly confusion.
Exchanging numbers. Arranging to keep in touch.

LITTLEBODY is number 23 in the Peppercanister
series by Thomas Kinsella. It is set in 12 point Times
New Roman and published in a paperback edition of
800 copies and a bound edition of 250 copies.

First published December 2000

The cover design is from a rubbing of a 15/16th century
carving of a piper on a stone formerly at Woodstock Castle.